SCOTNEY CASTLE
GARDEN

Kent

The National Trust

Scotney Castle Garden

Bluebells in the Scotney woods

The moated castle and landscape of Scotney compose an ideally romantic picture. The old buildings are of considerable architectural and historic interest, but it is the picture as a whole that is exceptional. This was created in the 1830s by Edward Hussey, who had the imagination to see how the medieval Scotney Castle could be transformed from derelict dwelling into quaint ruin, in order to form the focus of his new landscape garden. The result represents one of the last and most successful expressions of the Picturesque movement.

From the early 18th century, British landscape designers had been creating gardens inspired by pictures, but by 1800 a reaction had set in. Critics like the Rev. William Gilpin considered the grassy vistas designed by 'Capability' Brown too smooth and tidy; they might be beautiful, but they were not *picturesque*: to resemble the best landscape painting, a garden needed drama, variety and rough edges. At Scotney, the plunging site, the mixture of sheltered quarry and open lawn, and the ragged silhouette of the Old Castle provided all three in abundance.

Within the Picturesque composition devised by Edward Hussey, the planting has been enriched over a century and a half to emphasise bold shape and rich colour throughout the year. The Great Storm of 1987 shattered the picture, but the fallen cedars and cypresses have been replaced, and the newly exposed areas offer opportunities for experiment. While man-made gardens are always in a state of flux, the wild flowers, which are such an important part of the wider Scotney landscape, maintain their natural cycle.

Mixed azaleas in full bloom in springtime

The Old Castle; watercolour by John Piper, 1976 (detail)

The Early History of the Old Castle

The Darell lion crest

The secluded Scotney estate lies in the valley of the River Bewl on the Kent/Sussex border and has been inhabited since at least the 12th century. Roger Ashburnham built the castle *c*.1378–80, apparently in response to the threat of French invasion, although it was always more fortified manor house than fortress. Like nearby Bodiam Castle, it had circular towers at each corner, only one of which, the Ashburnham Tower, still stands; the foundations of the other three form the angles of the east island.

For 350 years Scotney Castle was the home of the Catholic Darell family, who rebuilt the south wing adjoining the Ashburnham Tower *c*.1580. In the early 17th century they hid the Jesuit Father Blount in the priest's hole which can still be seen in the Old Castle. Around 1640 William Darell demolished much of the castle, and used the masonry in a new three-storey east range, of which only the walls (bearing the lion crest of the Darells) are left. Around 1720 George Darell made further alterations, capping the Ashburnham Tower with a cupola and a conical tiled roof.

In the mid-18th century family squabbles led to lawsuits, which drained the Darells' resources and forced them to sell Scotney. In 1778 Edward Hussey bought the castle, and between 1783 and 1792 pieced the rest of the old Darell estate back together.

Scotney from the east, showing the three-storey range added in the 17th century and since mostly demolished; drawing made by Mark Vennet on 10 October 1783

The Old Castle in 1783; watercolour by Mark Vennet (detail)

The new house from below the quarry; watercolour by Edward Hussey, c.1845

Edward Hussey III, the creator of the garden, with his elder son, Edward Windsor, on the front steps of the new house around 1857

The Husseys
and the Creation of the Picturesque Garden

Edward Hussey (1749–1816) trained as a barrister, but was more interested in cricket than the law, playing frequently for the MCC from its foundation in 1787. His son, another Edward, survived him by only a year, leaving a widow, Ellen, who suspected that the castle's antiquated plumbing had killed them both. So she moved to St Leonards, where she brought up her son, Edward III (1809–94), who was fascinated from childhood by architecture and landscape gardening. In 1835 he decided to move back to Scotney and build a new house there.

A talented watercolourist influenced by the theories of the Picturesque movement, he approached the project with a picture-maker's eye. He sited his new home on a terrace 25 metres above the Old Castle, commissioning the architect Anthony Salvin to provide a country house with all mod. cons., but in a restrained Elizabethan style that used mellow sandstone quarried from the slope below. For advice on the planting, he turned to the Rev. Gilpin's nephew, William Sawrey Gilpin, who designed the area around the Bastion and devised the spectacular views down to the moat and the Old Castle, which was retained as a pleasantly jumbled ruin of different periods. Wooded parkland on the gently rising slope opposite provided a suitably arcadian backdrop.

Edward Hussey lived on until 1894, and so had the pleasure of seeing his planting reach full maturity. But by 1952, when his grandson Christopher inherited Scotney, the original design had inevitably become blurred by losses, and much of the surviving planting was past its best.

Christopher Hussey was an influential architectural writer with *Country Life* for over 50 years and the author of a pioneering study of the Picturesque (1927), which was inspired by his knowledge of Scotney. He saw as clearly as anyone that more radical and long-term planning was essential if the garden was to have a future, and he set this in train during the last eighteen years of his life. He was also keen that this unique creation should be enjoyed by others, and so decided to leave the estate to the National Trust on his death in 1970, in fulfilment of his unusually public-spirited family motto: *Vix ea nostra voco* ('I scarcely call these things our own'). His widow, Mrs Elizabeth (Betty) Hussey, and the National Trust have carried on this gradual renewal of the garden.

Christopher Hussey; painting by John Ward, 1964 (detail)

The Bastion and Top Walk

The semicircular balustraded Bastion offers the classic view down towards the castle ruins, seemingly enveloped in a sea of colourful foliage. As the Picturesque theorist Richard Payne Knight wrote in 1794:

Bless'd too is he, who, 'midst his tufted trees,
Some ruin'd castle's lofty towers sees;
Imbosom'd high upon the mountain's brow,
Or nodding o'er the stream that glides below.

The Great Storm of October 1987 brought down many of the mature Cedars of Lebanon, Scots Pines and Lawson Cypresses, which had provided the perfect frame for Edward Hussey's artful 'picture' of nature and history. Their replacements are rising with surprising speed and will eventually restore the vertical accents which are such an important part of the total composition.

The Top Walk is planted with such flowering trees and shrubs as magnolia, tulip tree, cistus and *Buddleja globosa*. It also reveals further views across the valley towards Goudhurst church on the opposite horizon. Closer at hand, climbing, floribunda and shrub roses surround a boldly carved Venetian font.

The Venetian font, which stands among roses opposite the lion's mouth fountain

The Old Castle from the Bastion in spring

The lion's mouth fountain

9

The Quarry and Main Lawn

Curving paths lead down from the Bastion to the quarry, which was a favourite element in the Picturesque landscape. As Payne Knight wrote in 1794:

The quarry long neglected, and o'ergrown
With thorns, that hang o'er mould'ring beds of stone,
May oft the place of nat'ral rocks supply,
And frame the verdant picture to the eye.

The planting in the Scotney quarry is, however, the result of careful thought rather than neglect. It is an ideally moist and shady home for many types of fern, including tall stands of Royal Fern. The large specimens of April-flowering *Magnolia stellata* are followed by the heavily scented Ghent azaleas in shades of yellow, cream and orange. They in turn are succeeded in high summer by hardy fuchsias and blue and white Willow Gentians.

From early in the year snowdrops, and then carpets of primroses and daffodils, cover the lawns that slope down towards the moat and the Old Castle. The massed clumps of *Ponticum* rhododendrons favoured by Picturesque garden designers come into their own in the spring.

Scotney is famous for its beds of *Kalmia latifolia*, which produce pink and white bell-like flowers in June. Late summer brings the intense blue tones of hydrangeas. Together with the rich autumnal reds and golds of nyssas, liquidambars and Japanese maples, they ensure a continual cycle of colour throughout the seasons.

The main lawns are home to large beds of *Kalmia latifolia*

A Ghent azalea

Ghent azalea 'Tricolour' in the Quarry Garden

The steps in the Quarry Garden are edged with Welsh poppies and ferns. A white Ghent azalea and an *Acer* form a canopy above

The Old Castle

The castle is a building that plays tricks with time. Paradoxically, the oldest part, the circular 14th-century Ashburnham Tower, is the best preserved, while the roofless east range, dating from 250 years later, is the most ruined. In early summer climbing roses, white wisteria, lilac and vines cover its walls in cheerful profusion. The borders around the castle are filled with shrub roses and herbaceous and bedding plants.

The American garden designer Lanning Roper, who advised on the planting at Scotney in the 1970s, laid out the little herb garden in a series of semicircular beds round the carved well-head, which was brought here by Christopher Hussey's aunt. Apart from many fragrant herbs, it features scented-leaved geraniums and heliotropes.

Round the edge of the moat and the stream that feeds it are numerous water-loving plants, including yellow irises in spring, further huge clumps of Royal Fern, which turn dark brown in autumn, and rodgersias, king-cups and forget-me-nots.

The Venetian well-head

Edward Hussey III's daughter Gertrude on the moat

The Old Castle from across the moat in spring

The Old Castle; watercolour by John Piper

The Moat and Ice-house

You emerge from the shade of the tree-lined Bridge Walk on to the little bridge that spans the neck of the moat. In the foreground to the left is the gabled wooden boathouse and beyond it the Ashburnham Tower reflected in the surrounding moat. From the opposite side of the bridge, one can take in the *Three Piece Reclining Figure – Draped* by Henry Moore, who was a friend of Christopher Hussey. In 1977 an isthmus was cleared of rhododendrons to provide a suitable setting, and the nearby planting has been kept deliberately simple: New Zealand flax, azaleas, ferns and the candelabra *Primula japonica* 'Postford White'.

The path between the south side of the moat and the River Bewl reveals another famous view: of the Old Castle in the foreground, contrasted with the gabled south-east corner of the new house on the horizon, as it rises from the quarry between trees. On the right is a grassy path which leads to the Chalybeate Spring. This produces water with a high iron content similar to that found in the nearby spa town of Tunbridge Wells.

At the north-east corner of the moat is the ice-house, a tent-shaped building thatched with heather. In the days before mechanical refrigeration, lumps of ice were taken from the moat in winter and stored here for use in the kitchen during the summer months.

Azaleas near the Moore statue

The ice-house

Three Piece Reclining Figure; by Henry Moore

The boathouse